THE ROAD TO VIRTUE

THE ROAD TO VIRTUE

RESOLUTIONS
FOR DAILY LIVING

Michael L. Loren, M.D.

AVON BOOKS NEW YORK

THE ROAD TO VIRTUE is an original publication of Avon Books. This work has never before appeared in book form.

AVON BOOKS
A division of
The Hearst Corporation
1350 Avenue of the Americas
New York, New York 10019

Copyright © 1996 by Michael Loren
Cover art by Al Pisano
Published by arrangement with the author
Library of Congress Catalog Card Number: 95-25565
ISBN: 0-380-78316-9

Library of Congress Cataloging in Publication Data:
Loren, Michael L.
   The road to virtue : resolutions for daily living / Michael Loren.
      p.   cm.
1. Conduct of life.   2. Virtues.   I. Title.
BJ1581.2.L68   1996   95-25565
179'.9—dc20   CIP

First Avon Books Trade Printing: April 1996

AVON TRADEMARK REG. U.S. PAT. OFF. AND IN OTHER COUNTRIES, MARCA REGISTRADA, HECHO EN U.S.A.

Printed in the U.S.A.

CW   10   9   8   7   6   5   4   3   2   1

To my wife, Ann,
and my children,
Rachel, Daniel, Rebecca, and Samuel,
with my love and affection

Akiva's greatest teacher—drops of water penetrating a rock

ACKNOWLEDGMENTS ∞

I want to acknowledge Beryl Wein, who educated me about the influence of Ben Franklin's *Autobiography* on European history and how ironic it was that Franklin's ideas never made it into the American home and classroom. My wife, Ann, as a school teacher, continually challenged me with the task of developing a method that could be used by individuals, parents, and teachers. Ed Christophersen suggested it is not enough to have inspirational ideas, but to include practical tasks that would actually implement the virtues. This manuscript would have never been completed without the encouragement and recommendations of my brother, Cary Loren. My sister, Jackie Lisiecki, made a number of important contributions that strengthen the manuscript.

I would like to especially thank my editor, Stephen S. Power, for his innumerable suggestions, patience, and insights. Finally, my parents, Sidney and Lillian Loren, always gave me encouragement and guidance.

Contents

🔷

THE ROAD TO VIRTUE

Introduction

So many of us are over-scheduled and stressed. We pursue happiness, but remain anxious, discouraged, and unfulfilled. Businesses are becoming meaner and leaner, and workers are becoming frustrated and burned out. Marriages and relationships are crumbling. A child trips a schoolmate for the fun of it. Many of us have lost hope, yet we look so happy and successful. Why are violence and addiction hidden so well? Why is so much sadness smiling?

Recently I found a comic strip that illustrated men rowing in a modern-day slave ship. A schedule listed the day's activities: 8 A.M. to 10 A.M. rowing, 10 A.M. to 12 P.M. rowing, 12 P.M. to 2 P.M. rowing ... etc. When I finished reading, I realized that we live our lives as though we were in the same boat. Like slaves we are forced to repeat certain actions. Often the worst ones. We fall into this trap at work, home, and school. Our days are habitual, organized, and without much freedom.

I wrote *The Road to Virtue* because I think we need a simple way of freeing ourselves. We need to ask ourselves: What counts? What values are important?

How do I conduct myself each day? Do I eat to live or do I live to eat? Do I live so I can see how many pistachio nuts I can stuff in my mouth? Is there more to life than just eating pistachio nuts?

The virtues developed by Benjamin Franklin suggest in an organized way how we can answer these questions and act to bring freedom into our lives. My hope is that by gradually improving ourselves we will all be happier and more successful with our friendships, family, and work.

In his autobiography, Franklin told a parable about a man who gave his axe to a blacksmith for sharpening and removal of speckling on the blade. As the axe was being ground, the man realized, "I think I like a speckled axe best." Franklin said, "A man without faults is a hateful creature. A good man should allow a few faults in himself, to keep his friends happy." We will always be speckled. Perhaps speckling adds some spice and variety. There will be many opportunities for us to slip and fall, but our failures and mistakes can be balanced with some optimism and humor. And, fortunately, there will be many more moments of happiness and success than failure.

The Road to Virtue

Benjamin Franklin was a publisher, printer, author, businessman, scientist, politician, and diplomat. He is known for *Poor Richard's Almanac*, scientific studies, and he signed both the Declaration of Independence and the United States Constitution. He wrote his autobiography to inspire and teach others, and it is still considered an important work.

But Franklin recognized that he also had shortcomings, and in his autobiography he offered readers a system of self-improvement, which he called the Art of Virtue. For example, Franklin loved telling jokes and puns; however, he felt he was spending too much of his time socializing and less time learning. He decided to focus on the virtue of Silence so as to gain knowledge. By actively trying to work on a particular problem, he was gradually able to improve himself.

For the sake of clarity, Franklin chose a large number of virtues that he considered universal and applicable to all people of all generations. He selected the virtues with some attention to their order. With Alertness he would gain knowledge, a benefit facilitated by Silence. He would need Order to accomplish actions, and Resolution to begin them. Conservation and Industry would follow from the resolve to waste nothing and be useful. The first six virtues, beginning with Alertness and ending with Industry, can serve as a framework for building an organization, solving a problem, or improving a relationship. The virtues of Sincerity and Justice would allow us to form relationships that would be more easily accomplished with Conservation and Industry. Moderation would serve as a balance to all the virtues. The additional virtues of Health, Calmness, Friendship, and Modesty would add warmth and sensitivity to the other virtues.

Franklin developed a specific system for working on the virtues. He kept a "little book" or diary, and on each page he wrote out a particular virtue with a few short phrases to explain it. For example, regarding Silence, he wrote, "Speak not what may benefit others or yourselves. Avoid trifling Conversation." On each page were also listed other virtues. Franklin kept a tally of any errors or mistakes he may have made with any virtue for a particular week, but in general he would focus on one main virtue per week. Franklin wrote, "Like him who having a Garden to weed, does not attempt to eradicate all the bad herbs at once, which would exceed his Reach and his Strength, but works on one of the Beds at a time."

Franklin would start each morning with the question, "What good shall I do today?" and end each day in the evening with the question, "What good have I done today?" Since he worked on himself each day, he eventually was able to write, "I was supriz'd to find myself so much full of faults than I had imagined. But I had the satisfaction of seeing them diminish."

Franklin developed the Art of Virtue as a teaching tool also. He believed that the Art of Virtue could be taught to children like the piano or science, and he meant for people to incorporate these lessons into their daily living to help them become better individuals. He felt these lessons could also guide their actions, improving those as well. If individuals could improve, that is, take responsibility for their actions and recognize they always have the opportunity to change, then society would be the beneficiary.

Franklin's intention of writing and publishing his Art of Virtue was never accomplished during his lifetime. With some regret, Franklin blamed his lack of industry in this matter to ever-pressing private business during the early part of his life and to his extensive public business toward the end of it. He clearly viewed this as a "great and extensive Project that remain'd unfinish'd."

Franklin's 13 virtues may have been his greatest work. They served as the tools that made him such a great man. I suspect that they also motivated men like Washington, Jefferson, and Madison. In a sense, these virtues carved the cornerstones and dug the foundation upon which the United States was built. It is ironic that they never made it into the educational system of the United States. I think that now more than any time before, they are very much needed.

I am concerned that we are not meeting our educational goals. Schools are being overloaded with misbehaving and disrespectful children. I am especially concerned about the increasing use of illegal drugs and violence in our cities and schools. In Kansas City, one out of eight African-American adolescent males will be shot or killed by the time they reach their eighteenth birthday. Many children are often left to their own devices, through which they develop their own system of values. Television and uneducated peers have often taken over the roles traditionally managed by parents. We need to teach our children character as well as facts and figures. For that, according to Martin Luther King, Jr., is the goal of true education.

Thus, with some of the virtues' names modernized, I am presenting Franklin's Art of Virtue in a form that all of us can use. Each of the 13 virtues is elucidated with quotations from men and women of different historical time periods, religions, ethnicity, professions, and cultures, proving that the virtues Franklin wrote of are truly timeless and universal concerns.

We are living in a difficult time. Our social fabric seems to be unraveling. There appear to be some cracks in the foundation of this country. I think that these virtues may serve as a key to repairing some of the damage.

How Do I Get Started?

Many of us do not have time to read a book from cover to cover. It is rare for us to find a few free minutes. But even if you only had one minute free each day, you could accomplish much. This book is designed for a fast read, for the grazer-type of reader. For each virtue I've given readers a brief description of the virtue, followed by some quotations with reflective comments, suggested actions for implementing the virtue, and additional quotations. Try to read a chapter, a page, or a quote each day. Repetition, however, is the key to success. One step follows another step that will begin a trip that ends 1000 miles away. If possible, keep a journal as Franklin did. It will offer constant encouragement by showing you've progressed, as well as serve as a constant reminder that there is more work to be done. Do you have a special time when you might reflect? Good times might be early in the morning for a few minutes, at breakfast, during your lunch break, or just before you go to sleep. Think about the virtues during your commute, while you're washing dishes, as you brush your teeth. Think about them during all those times when you might not be thinking at all.

I wrote this book to help bridge generation gaps—to share with a child or grandchild. I believe that we have a responsibility to pass on this knowledge to future generations. Adolescents and teenagers will be able to read *The Road to Virtue*. Suggest to them that it will give them insights on developing leadership skills and prepare them for success in the workforce. Ask them to review a section of it, then ask them what they thought. What quotes did they enjoy? What are the advantages and disadvantages of each virtue? Which virtues did they think might be difficult to put into practice? When I have weekly discussions with my children, I find it useful to sit in a quiet living room, with the television off and the answering machine on. I will often discuss what happened to me over the last few days. Sometimes I will discuss a newspaper story illustrating a person with a good character or virtues. It may sound crass, but I tie my children's allowance to having our weekly discussions. As children mature, they will be attracted to virtues for the sake of the virtues. When the child is younger, however, I think they respond better with small bribes of candy, clothes, and money. This is a timeless strategy that works.

Simply posting a quote a day, defining the words, and explaining the quote may be a simple way of introducing virtues to a classroom. Frequently the daily newspaper, weekly magazines, and even the comics will have examples that facilitate the discussion. In a classroom, more time may be needed for group discussions about actual situations or current events that may apply to a particular virtue or character trait. Classroom writing exercises can focus on particular virtues. And there are always moments when a virtue can be presented after someone is disruptive, makes a mess, picks a fight, or neglects to do an assignment. Repetition and daily study is especially helpful for young children so the virtues can become a part of their nature. And children learn virtues by modeling their behavior after their parents' and teachers' actions, so it is not enough for us to tell them how to be good. We also have to do the right thing. Virtues can be taught to children as young as three or four years old. Of course many of the quotations and ideas may have to be modified so young children will understand them. For more details about using this in the classroom, see the appendix, "10 Ways to Use *The Road to Virtue* in the Classroom."

In the workplace, there are serious problems that undercut the effectiveness of employees: nasty co-workers, gossip, burnout, anger, poor crisis management, poor communication, unclear job responsibilities, and a lack of recognition. We also need to realize that problems at home will frequently find their way into the workplace. Franklin's 13 virtues can also be used in the workplace as a method for improving the character and effectiveness of employees, helping prevent problems, and augmenting employees' skills. *The Road to Virtue* can also add value to existing programs of Job Orientation for new employees, Conflict Resolution, Diversity in the Workplace, Human Resource Counseling, and Leadership Training. By enabling each employee to be a success, the virtues can make an entire business a success.

All the virtues should be reviewed frequently. It is not enough just to learn them once and then never to study them again. It is amazing how short our memories can be. Franklin's virtues might be viewed as a discipline. Just as we need discipline to train as a competitive athlete or professional musician, we also must practice regularly to improve our skills as a human being. Hopefully, over time, most of the 13 virtues can be integrated into our actions while at home, school, or work.

Ultimately the virtues need to be converted into good actions. I've suggested a few; I hope you enjoy coming up with some more. Perhaps you could do one per week, a test of all you've learned. Did you succeed? How did you feel? And evaluate your performance honestly. Then do the action again.

Each of the 13 virtues has many ways of being viewed, like a diamond with different facets. For each virtue there are quotations that can give you a somewhat different perspective on it. Many of the virtues seem to overlap; qualities of one may be found in another. Also some quotations may be used for more than one virtue. All the virtues share the same underlying theme, though: Be a responsible caring person. This is probably the essence of what Franklin was trying to accomplish during his life.

THE FIRST VIRTUE
Alertness

In his early years, Ben Franklin wrote about his intoxicated coworkers and resolved not to waste his time or money on drinking. Instead he chose to make something of himself. He knew that if he kept a "coolness and clearness of head," then he could become educated and would have more success in pursuing all the other qualities that he wanted to develop. Thus he made Alertness his first virtue.

Often Alertness involves knowing who your friends are and knowing when you are over your head. When he was seventeen years old, Franklin was ambitious. He desperately wanted his own print shop. The prominent governor of Pennsylvania enticed him to do just that. His father felt that at his young age, Ben needed more experience and it was a foolish governor that was misleading his son. Sure enough, Franklin would later be severely embarrassed by the governor, who made elaborate promises of financial backing without real substance. This experience taught Franklin to be more cautious and knowledgeable about his relationships. New acquaintances may often appear to have our best interest at heart. We need to be cautious and listen to their words carefully, and we need to build a gradual trust and respect for them based on their good deeds, not their promises or flashy dress.

Alertness also consists of viewing the world with thought, enthusiasm, and imagination. There are moments of intense awe that can inspire us: the smile of a child, beautiful music, or the vastness of the Grand Canyon. These moments can take our breath away and inspire us. There are simple wonderful things that we encounter each day that can have that same magic effect provided we develop this virtue.

Alertness requires flexibility and preparedness. We need to anticipate problems and plan ahead until we "see it done." For example, if I picture myself swinging a bat and making contact with the ball, I've increased the chance that my real swing will result in a hit.

Alertness is the first step to becoming a productive problem solver. There are always situations at home and work that allure us, test us, and trip us up. It is important that we stay alert so we do not fall into traps set up by others or ourselves and so we can see a way around them.

You can't depend on your judgment when your imagination is out of focus.

—MARK TWAIN

———————————

We shouldn't be so sure of ourselves. Even plans we think are perfect may be dead wrong because we often make assumptions based on incomplete or misread information, then act to our worst advantage. If we check and double-check our facts, we may be able to improve our judgment. In addition, some of us may need an attitude adjustment before we can think clearly.

The educated differ from the uneducated as much as the living from the dead.

—ARISTOTLE

———————

It is not always obvious who is educated or uneducated. An education based on careful thought and analysis is more valuable than one based on memorization alone. Someone who reads all the classics of literature because they happen to be classics isn't necessarily educated. There is an ancient question: Who is wise? Usually we answer by saying it is a person who knows a lot or who is a great teacher. However, consider the answer to be that a wise person is someone who can learn from anyone. Great lessons can be learned from even a small child. We can learn a great deal by just studying the simple ant. To gain wisdom is an active lifetime process.

I have a dream that one day this nation will rise up and live out the true meaning of its creed: *"We hold these truths to be self-evident; that all men are created equal."*

—MARTIN LUTHER KING, JR.

———————————

King displays a clarity of thought and an ability to envision the future he hoped to create. Given all his efforts, that day may occur tomorrow. But possibly our nation is still asleep or ignoring certain truths. Perhaps each of us also needs a dream as a guide for our actions—to make them as powerful as Dr. King's. So that our nation will rise up and live.

Better an empty purse than an empty head.

—GERMAN PROVERB

Having no money is usually a temporary thing, and with work we can earn a living. An empty head is more difficult to change. Provided we are willing to open our minds and listen and learn, we may be able to overcome our ignorance. The question is, what do we want to fill our heads with? MTV? Nintendo? *The National Inquirer*? If our heads are filled with nonsense or misinformation, they can be worse than empty. I look for information that I think will be helpful for myself and others. If a piece of information will simplify my life, improve my communication with others, and give me a sense of peace, I find it valuable.

Men are not prisoners of fate, but only prisoners of their own minds.

—FRANKLIN D. ROOSEVELT

———————————

How often do we complain and scream about what is happening to us instead of realizing that we can often control what is occurring? Fate seems so unavoidable, but it does not have to be so! We need to escape from negative thoughts and feelings of helplessness. Freedom from a prison of the mind may seem far off in the distance. However, it is really just a thought away.

WHAT TO DO ∞

1. *Go to the library.* The main point of being alert is to be educated. Beginning in his childhood, Franklin had a thirst for knowledge. He loved to read books, and he would spend any money he saved on them. He would set aside time at night and in the early morning for reading. When he became older and prosperous, he started the first free public library system in Philadelphia. Use your local library, perhaps the greatest and most underrated community resource. From books you can get a wonderful education; and librarians are skilled in directing you toward good writers and periodicals.

2. *Find a mentor.* In the business community many people learn and advance under the wings of a mentor. Older or retired teachers, professionals, and business people who have had many years of life experience can be an invaluable resource. Attend free community lectures and conferences. The local chamber of commerce can also be an excellent resource. Interview your potential mentor and ask about his/her successes and failures. Is this someone with whom you would feel comfortable sharing your own private questions? Is he/she interested in seeing you succeed? Mentors can be found in a neighbor, minister, coach, or classmate. Look for character qualities that you might admire and emulate. Your mentor may also serve as your role model. You may find two or three persons who can serve as mentors.

3. *Examine how you are spending your time.* We often get so tied up in our careers, events, and television shows that we don't leave time for doing the things that really are important. We often are so badly over-scheduled and stressed-out that we don't have time to think about what we really want to be doing. So turn off the television and telephone for one evening each week and think about how you really want to spend your time. Then start doing it.

4. *Don't depend on alcohol and drugs for relaxation.* Alcohol and drugs tend to dull the mind and interfere with any sense of alertness. There are many healthy ways to relax without potentially dangerous medical and mental side effects: walking, jogging, yoga, afternoon naps, hobbies, and meditation, for example. These activities offer you clarity of thought and a safe endorphin high.

ADDITIONAL QUOTES ON ALERTNESS ∞

The mere imparting of information is not education. Above all things, the effort must result in making a man think and do for himself.

—CARTER G. WOODSON

_____

_____

_____

_____

_____

Knowledge is like a garden: if it is not cultivated it cannot be harvested.

—GUINEA PROVERB

_____

_____

_____

Armed with the knowledge of our past, we can with confidence charter a course for our future.

—MALCOLM X

_____

_____

_____

Pain makes man think. Thought makes man wise. Wisdom makes life endurable.

—JOHN PATRICK

_____

_____

_____

The doors of the world are open to people who can read.

—SONYA CARSON

_____

_____

_____

Silence

Franklin described himself as having a habit of "prattling, punning, and joking," but he also understood the value of silence. He wrote, "Silence would be more easy, and my desire being to gain knowledge, knowledge ... was obtained rather by the use of the ears than of the tongue." In addition, Franklin knew that when we do speak, we should do so economically, that is, "Say little, do much." In his later years in Congress, serving as a representative from Pennsylvania, Franklin rarely spoke in public, but rather accomplished things behind the scenes. So while not noted for his oratory, he was recognized as a leader of immense wisdom.

Silence can also be misused. Clearly there are times when we need to speak out to defend a person or a situation. Our words can rescue someone in distress. And if we don't speak against what we feel is wrong, then often our silence may be interpreted as agreement with what was said or done.

The popular childhood expression "Sticks and stones may break my bones but names will never hurt me," is untrue. When someone hits me, it hurts, but the injury will heal over time. A malicious word, however, can attack my very essence and scar me for the rest of my life. People might defend themselves by saying, "But it is true!" Even when we speak the truth, we can still harm another. According to Franklin, we should "speak not but what may benefit others." Words need to be used with some thought and tact, and often the kindest word is the unspoken one. Gossip, sarcasm, and cut-downs at times may appear innocent. A cut-down, however, is just a way of making ourselves seem bigger at another's expense. This is not a nice way to act.

A good goal is to use few words to convey great ideas. Teachers need to teach in a direct, simple fashion rather than by using complicated, convoluted phrasing. Their goal is to make difficult ideas easy to understand. If the words are many and the essence is little, this is folly. It is also wise not to speak for such a long time. There is an old expression that says a fool's voice comes with an abundance of words.

A proverb states that wisdom is protected by silence. Often when we interrupt another person's speech, we may not get the full message and we may not learn properly. Our listening skills often need to be developed. We have two ears and one mouth. Another good goal is to use our ears more than our mouths.

It is easy to utter what has been kept silent, but impossible to recall what has been uttered.

—PLUTARCH

———————

Nasty hurtful thoughts can be turned into words easily. We have a responsibility to be careful with our speech. Once a word is spoken, it cannot be taken back.

There is an old story of a man who embarrassed his best friend with words of gossip spoken to other people. Later he attempted to apologize to the friend. He was told that he could repair what he did by emptying a pillow full of feathers in the wind and then collecting every feather. It was probably an easier task collecting the feathers than retracting what had been said.

Talk does not cook rice.

—JAPANESE PROVERB

––––––––––––––

This is another way of saying, Actions speak louder than words. My wife is a teacher and frequently uses this proverb when a student continually chatters away and steals time from the class. When the children hear the proverb, they quickly are reminded to stop talking and focus.

There often comes a time when we need to stop discussion and get on with a task. Rice and talk are both needed for survival. With rice we feed our belly. With talk we feed our soul. Without rice, though, our souls are not worth much even with a lot of talk. Look at the poverty and starvation surrounding us in the United States. Despite all the talk, there is still a great deal of work to be done.

The world in silence nods, but my heart weeps.

—CLAUDE McKAY

Silence can be used in a positive way to learn and improve communication; however, many times it can have devastating effects. Listen to the silence while an elderly person dies of loneliness. Listen to the painful silence when brothers refuse to talk for years because of a trivial misunderstanding. Listen to the silent screams as we watch millions die of starvation or watch refugees turned away from freedom.

To speak without thinking is to shoot without aiming.

—SPANISH PROVERB

We need to know our words can be as dangerous as bullets and to be cautious in how we phrase them. In some situations it is much wiser to have no opinion or to keep our opinions to ourselves. I have regretted speaking many more times than I have regretted my silence, for often when I speak without much thought, I end up shooting myself in the foot.

WHAT TO DO ∞

1. *Give others time to say what they have to say.* Sometimes if I don't respond immediately, and pause in my speech, the other person may say more and reveal what is really important.

2. *Speak little and do much.* Don't make too many promises. Surprise the other person by doing more than is expected. I once saw this sign at a car rental place: "Don't promise the customer more than you can deliver and deliver more than you promise."

3. *Speak up when you witness an apparent injustice.* Often it is easy not getting involved. After all, we are all busy—and who has the time to help out someone in trouble? If we don't get involved, though, we are tacitly approving the injustice. First examine the situation. Then, if after weighing the evidence you believe that a wrong has occurred, write letters to newspapers, congressmen, and senators, asking for their support. Let the person or group being treated unjustly know you're on their side. Ask what you can do to help. You may need to involve other friends and give of your time and money to help solve the problem.

4. *Be sensitive to how you speak of others.* Gossiping about other people is a difficult habit to break. Hearing a baby scream makes many of us want to leave the room; we need to react to gossip in a similar fashion. You might change the topic if someone tries to gossip with you. You might tell them directly, "I don't feel comfortable gossiping." Or you might turn the conversation into a way to help the person. For example, you might say, "I am sorry that Jan is getting a divorce, I think that this will be a rough time for her. Is there anything I can do to help?"

5. *Don't speak until your anger has subsided.* When I am angry and I correct my child, I find it better not to speak at that moment but to delay what I have to say until I have a clearer head, perhaps later that day. I am reminded of a saying that stops me in my tracks when I get angry with my child: An angry person loses his brains. I can't stand the idea of my brains falling out in front of my child.

ADDITIONAL QUOTES ON SILENCE ∞

It is better to keep your mouth shut and appear stupid than to open it and remove all doubt.

—MARK TWAIN

_____

_____

_____

_____

_____

Even doubtful accusations leave a stain behind them.

—THOMAS FULLER, M.D.

_____

_____

_____

Silence is not always golden; tact is golden, not silence.

—SAMUEL BUTLER

_____

_____

_____

A silent tongue does not betray its owner.

—AFRICAN PROVERB

_____

_____

_____

_____

_____

Order

According to Franklin, order was the virtue most difficult for him to master. Although he was brilliant, he often had many irons in his fire, and it was hard for him to decide which task should be worked on and completed first. Franklin eventually learned what each of us should: "Let all your things have their places. Let each part of your business have its time."

Fortunately Franklin could depend on his capable wife, Deborah, to keep his business dealings in order. She was invaluable in running the day-to-day operations of his printing business.

The way we conduct and organize our day determines if we will be able to complete tasks successfully. It may also affect our health. A few years ago a woman introduced me to day-planners, sharing with me an incredible story about how a day-planner saved her husband's life. Because of his poor organizational skills, he was floundering at work, in fear of losing his job, and contemplating suicide. He was becoming anxious and depressed. And now his whole life has turned right-side up just because he was able to get his time in control.

Are there extremes of being too orderly or having a lack of order? Certainly! Often I get so wrapped up in the method of doing something, the task doesn't get completed.

It is much easier doing one task at a time. Often when we attempt to work on two or three projects simultaneously, we accomplish nothing—or, worse, we end up ruining all of them.

When Franklin first developed his system of self-improvement, he wrote it down in a small book. When he became older, he did not need to refer to the book as much; however, he still kept it with him for periodic review and to serve as a reminder of the important ideals and priorities that he valued. He knew from experience there are times when we get off track and focus on the wrong projects.

Order is the shape upon which beauty depends.

—PEARL S. BUCK

Which order? There are as many methods of ordering as there are turns in our imaginations. Consider the way I organize my small room: If I can make order from relentless chaos for even a moment, then I have created beauty. And this beauty may relax me and give me peace. Order is often temporary, though, and just as a rose wilts and crumbles, the order in my room may collapse and require some attention.

"Begin at the beginning," the king said gravely, *"and go till you come to the end; then stop."*

—LEWIS CARROLL

"Begin at the beginning ..." Where else should we begin? To begin a task you have to start with a plan. Otherwise you may overlook critical steps and fail. And if it is an important task, begin slowly, "gravely," and proceed with cautious steps. Every project has an ending. Do not drag it out needlessly. Complete it, then go on to a new project.

Ill habits gather by unseen degrees, as brooks make rivers, rivers run to seas.

—OVID

————————————

Bad habits often creep up on us without our being aware of them. They often begin innocently in our childhood, learned from our parents, siblings, television, and friends; then with repetition, they become a part of our nature. Parents need to recognize the profound impact they can have on their children, and that it is never too early to begin guiding their child in the right direction. There is a story of a man who went to a teacher and asked when he should teach the virtues to his three-year-old. The teacher replied frantically, "Hurry, run home, you may be too late."

There is a best way of doing everything. If it be to boil an egg.

—RALPH WALDO EMERSON

Even boiling an egg requires some initial instruction and guidance. Every action we take can be accomplished in several ways. But how do we know if what has always been done is really the best way? Maybe you can develop a new way of doing something, even if it is only to boil an egg.

WHAT TO DO ∽

1. _Keep a journal or day-planner._ Ben Franklin kept a "little book" in which he listed his virtues and what he would do each day. In a sense he developed his own day-planner. He felt that his book kept his goals in front of him, thereby enabling him to focus on improving his habits and also to keep better track of his daily affairs. And by planning out each day, he felt he could accomplish more. For the last five years I have been using a day-planner, which I take everywhere. Recently I had it waterproofed so I could use it in the shower.

2. _Create strategies._ Franklin was addicted to chess, a game based on strategy and order. To play well requires looking ahead, planning, and stringing together 'what if' scenarios. This is how you can approach difficult problems—by breaking them down into smaller parts and approaching them one at a time. At times you may have to adjust your plan due to changing conditions. Don't get discouraged, though; victory may not be far away.

3. _Make lists of what you want to accomplish._ A list of long-term goals and short-term goals can be helpful. Long-term goals are things that you may want to be doing at home or work in a few years from now—for example, a change of occupation, or involvement in a social organization such as the Boy Scouts. Short-term goals may involve planning a canoe trip with your family this summer, or learning a foreign language by the end of the year.

4. *Clutter may slow you down.* At times you may have to put your house in order. I am frequently tripping over stacks of paper in my living room. My wife continually reminds me to do something with piles of medical journals, or she will find a new home for them in the trash. I get especially frustrated looking for misplaced papers. Slowly I am learning to put things away in files. And if I finish reading a journal, rather than stack it, I now discard it.

ADDITIONAL QUOTES ON ORDER ∽

Out of intense complexities intense simplicities emerge.

—WINSTON CHURCHILL

_____

_____

_____

_____

_____

Without oars, you cannot cross in a boat.

—JAPANESE PROVERB

_____

_____

_____

_____

_____

ORDER — 45

Order marches with weighty and measured strides; disorder is always in a hurry. . . . We often get in quicker by the back door than by the front.

—NAPOLEON I

_____

_____

_____

_____

_____

Amid a multitude of projects, no plan is devised. . . . It is a bad plan that admits no modification.

—PUBLILIUS SYRUS

_____

_____

_____

_____

_____

Resolution

Ben Franklin was very creative. He had dozens of ideas and plans going through his brain every day. After he conceived a project, he arranged all the items necessary to make it a success; and then he put his energy into the project until he completed it. Although there were many problems which he had to face. But he was bull-headed in his desire to succeed, and he would not allow a lack of money to get in the way of his goals.

Franklin gave up his work as a printer, spent much of his money, and devoted four years of his life to do experiments day and night to unravel the mysteries of electricity. He created terms such as battery, plus and minus charges, and conductor. Despite the dangers of the experiments, Franklin resolved to continue his work and made the incredible discovery that lightning and electricity were the same thing. His discovery catapulted him into instant international fame.

Later Franklin served as a representative for the colonies in England. After the Boston Tea Party, he was severely embarrassed by the English government, which had begun putting the screws to the colonies. Franklin saw all his work as a diplomat go down the drain. This was a major turning point in his life, and he decided to leave England and return to America. Franklin resolved that his main goal now was to offer leadership to the colonists and to prepare for war against England.

Franklin could speak from experience when he said, "Resolve to perform what you ought. Perform without fail what you resolve." Consult your advisors, create plans, focus our energies, and complete it. Sometimes, however, our mentors may be unable to advise us, our goals may be uncertain, or our course of action blocked. Other times we may have to act despite lingering doubts or a desire to hesitate. And there is always the chance that something will go wrong with even our best laid plans. These frustrations happen to everyone. In these cases, we need to pick ourselves up, refocus, and start again—fresh and confident.

Remember: Valuable discoveries and worthwhile projects do not come easily. Failure is common. In science most laboratory experiments fail, but scientists often learn a great deal from their mistakes. Edison said, "Genius is 1 percent inspiration and 99 percent perspiration." He should know. He tested thousands of materials before he developed the first tungsten electric lamp.

Fleming capitalized on an apparent failed experiment to discover the antibiotic penicillin. If it wasn't for their resolve to work through failure, Franklin, Edison, Fleming, and thousands of other scientists would never have made such wonderful discoveries.

You may be disappointed if you fail, but you are doomed if you don't try.

—BEVERLY SILLS

———————

If I fail I will be disappointed—I want to succeed. But a disappointment does not have to become a lingering feeling of failure. There is always the opportunity to try again, but if I never try, how can I possibly succeed? So I take a chance and act. I often counsel patients to stop smoking. Many fear trying to stop because they fear failing. Others get discouraged by the comments and looks of relatives or friends. And some just need a few words of encouragement to guide them down the road of success. Usually after I first advise people to stop smoking, months and even years will pass before the patients do something. In their hearts they know quitting is the correct thing to do; however, they still have not resolved to do it. I think once they start, their fear of failure is easily overcome.

Parents can only give good advice or put them on the right paths, but the final forming of a person's character lies in their own hands.

—ANNE FRANK

No matter how good your parents' advice was, you may have nonetheless deviated from the path they had intended. Many of us are carrying heavy baggage of anger and resentments against our parents from our childhood. What if your parents didn't care about you? What if they gave you bad advice? What if you are now on the wrong path? Although you may end up falling in the attempt, you can still find the right path. It may not be an easy task. We all have weak qualities that could stand improvement, and we've all made poor decisions. Don't blame unfortunate circumstances, however, on your parents. Accept that the future is really in your hands. We can do a great deal, provided we resolve to make it a priority. You might start by making peace with yourself and your parents. This peace offering can often release you so you can achieve and make real progress.

If you wish to learn the highest truth, you must begin with the alphabet.

—JAPANESE PROVERB

Sometimes difficult problems can be solved when they are reduced to their components, just as we learn a language by first learning its alphabet. We may need to work slowly on each component before we can reach the larger solution. Perhaps the alphabet in the proverb also symbolizes innocence. With the resolve to approach a task with the excitement of a child, we can overcome obstacles. Sometimes our sophistication may complicate the data and hinder our success.

Habit is habit, and not to be flung out of the window by any man, but coaxed downstairs a step at a time.

—MARK TWAIN

———————

It is a slow process to lose bad habits and to take on good ones. If we move too quickly, these changes will not stick. Stay on track and have patience; things will improve. It takes a great deal of courage to follow a path of improvement. There may be many discouragements. There may be times when we will fall down. But just as quickly as we may fall off track, we have the ability to snap back, perhaps wiser for the experience.

WHAT TO DO ∽

1. *Don't let your "to do" list sit.* Procrastination is a difficult habit to break, and distasteful tasks are often hard to start. Putting them on a list is a good first step. But a next step still needs to be taken. I find myself assigning distasteful tasks a high priority, then too often passing over them quickly and focusing on the trivial stuff for the day. Today put aside your minor tasks and tackle your toughest problems.

2. *Seek advice.* Difficult challenges may seem insurmountable. Many of us would more readily try something new if we had more encouragement from family and friends, but often these people try to discourage us instead. When your resolve wavers, discuss the challenge with people who have successfully done what you are planning to do. They will be able to warn you about any mistakes others have made, and their own success will bolster your spirit.

3. *Don't get distracted.* Stress, conflicts, and problems at home, school, or work interfere with our ability to act. A worthwhile but difficult skill is being able to tune out these distractions so you can successfully complete the task at hand.

Many people use humor to alleviate tension, so take a break to laugh. Every morning I make a point to read the comics in the paper. Actually for me this is the high point. You can also manage bothersome thoughts with deep breathing, physical activity, and relaxation training, which might include meditation, yoga, and prayer. These skills do not always come naturally and may require practice.

4. *Be open to making improvements.* Frequently we all honestly intend to make major improvements in our habits at home or work or to try something new. We may just as frequently find it difficult to follow through. A revolution, however, may begin with simply a small modification to what we have been doing. I often counsel sedentary patients to exercise regularly, and many just roll their eyes, imagining having to join an elaborate exercise club and lots of sweating. Instead I suggest they just walk five minutes away from their home and return. Gradually they may be able to devote more time to a walk and convert a discouraging activity into something they look forward to each day.

ADDITIONAL QUOTES ON RESOLUTION ⬲

Do not be afraid of the past. If people tell you that it is irrevocable, do not believe them.

—OSCAR WILDE

_____

_____

_____

_____

_____

What may be done at any time will be done at no time.

—THOMAS FULLER

_____

_____

_____

_____

_____

Many persons have a wrong idea of what constitutes true happiness. It is not attained through self-gratification, but through fidelity to a worthy purpose.

—HELEN KELLER

_____

_____

_____

_____

_____

Success is the result of perfection, hard work, learning from failure, loyalty, and persistence.

—COLIN POWELL

_____

_____

_____

Courage is contagious. When a brave man takes a stand, the spines of others are stiffened.

—BILLY GRAHAM

_____

_____

_____

Conservation

Conservation has traditionally focused on saving land, water, resources, and energy. But time is also a commodity, perhaps our most precious, and there never seems to be enough of it.

I find myself starving from a lack of time. Often I am terribly over-committed to people, committees, and activities and need far more than twenty-four hours in a day to complete what I have to do. It is so easy getting caught in a swamp of nonsense and trivia. We all need one day each week when we turn off the phones and television and recharge our batteries. It can be a day spent recognizing the beauty in our friends, family, and the world around us. It's a day like this that gives our time on earth value.

Also Franklin said, "Make no expense but to do good to others or yourself." Waste nothing. When Franklin was seven years old, he bought a small whistle from a visiting child for all the pocket change he had. However, when he soon realized that he had paid four times more than what the whistle was really worth, he became greatly disturbed and the whistle suddenly lost its charm. This episode had a profound effect on him. Later, when purchasing something, he would frequently remind himself to be frugal by saying, "Don't pay too much for that whistle." Franklin generalized this principle of "paying too much for that whistle" to all that he valued, including his relationships and how he chose to spend his time.

If we do not have enough time and money for everyone and everything, then we must first take care of the needs of ourselves and family before reaching out to our friends and our community. Recently I met a minister who said he needed to focus on, support, and strengthen his own family before he would be able to effectively help members of his own congregation. If his own house was in disarray, this would adversely undercut his effectiveness in leading his congregation. At times, of course, my selfish needs serve as an excuse not to help others. Obviously a balance needs to be met.

Managing our time commitments requires prioritizing what we are doing. To use our time effectively, we need to put some order into how we spend our time.

Simplicity, simplicity, simplicity! I say, let your affairs be as two or three, and not a hundred or a thousand; instead of a million count half a dozen, and keep your accounts on your thumb-nail.

—HENRY DAVID THOREAU

We are living in a complicated age with busy schedules, cable television, instant news, and an overload of information, but you can avoid being overwhelmed. Work at keeping things simple. Cut down on the commitments. Prioritize! Schedule free time. Take less work home. Go out more. If you imagine your life is killing you, it's time to focus on what is truly necessary—and these are often life's simplest pleasures.

I believe we would be happier to have a personal revolution in our individual lives and go back to simpler living and more direct thinking. It is the simple things in life that make living worthwhile, the sweet fundamental things such as love and duty, work and rest and living close to nature.

—LAURA INGALLS WILDER

In addition to recognizing the value of our time on earth, we need to realize the value of other people's lives. We have a responsibility to care for the deserted and the lonely, the elderly and the infirm. The lives of millions of adults and children are being ignored and wasted each day. It seems easier for me to talk about the millions of people starving in Africa than for me to talk about a single sick, elderly neighbor. True, I cannot take care of everyone, but I can help those around me.

The biggest disease today is not leprosy or tuberculosis, but rather the feeling of being unwanted, uncared for and deserted by everyone.

—MOTHER TERESA

Why do people have these feelings of loneliness? Do I contribute to them? How can I cure them? And am I or my family infected? If I only pursue happiness for myself, will I still be sensitive to others' unhappiness? If I am only for myself, what am I?

Loneliness is not a disease that can be pointed to and controlled with money and technology like leprosy or tuberculosis. Only by offering our hearts, our hands, and our time to others can we cure it.

The ability to simplify means to eliminate the unnecessary so that the necessary may speak.

—HANS HOFMANN

Often noise and complication hide the truth. We are trapped with conflicting ideas that confuse us and steal our time. I have to read hundreds of pages of journals each month, and so much of it is junk information. Many of the articles are unnecessarily complex, which is an attempt to hide irrelevant information. I frequently need to develop filters to strain out the information so I can uncover what I will find usable. I focus on certain topics that I have an interest in and gravitate to information that is clearly written and easily understood. Usually I end up scanning articles and briefly looking over summaries.

When I am counseling patients, frequently I give them so much information that they are confused and overloaded and leave my office unsure of what they need to be doing. Sometimes less is best and giving them just a few directions and short explanations provides them with enough clarity to understand what is necessary.

WHAT TO DO ∞

1. *Devote your time and money to community service.* I have seen successful businessmen, lawyers, doctors, and others spend time with their own children and other children in worthwhile programs such as Big Brothers, Boys and Girls Club, and scouting, and not only have an impact on others, but also gain a great deal of personal satisfaction from what they were adding to society. There are many service and religious organizations that need volunteers to work in hospitals, hospices, and nursing facilities. Volunteers are desperately needed to assist teachers in public schools. Adults are needed to teach the millions of adults in America who are illiterate. And many of these programs will train you in return.

2. *Be a mentor.* Youths of the inner cities are often discouraged because of a lack of opportunities and a lack of hope. Many children learn their ethics from the street. Mentors are needed to help guide these children in the proper direction. Not uncommonly, they need to realize that there are responsible adults available who really care about them and who can give them time, love, and advice. These children can be rescued if we act now.

3. *Conserve your money.* Franklin wanted people to use their financial resources in a prudent fashion. With a solid financial base, we become less of a burden on society and can then give back to society. What can you do? Buy a modest car. Live in a home that will not stretch you with high monthly payments. Try to avoid buying items with credit cards unless you can pay off the balance each month. When buying clothing, go after classic styles that will not go out of style, and get quality so the clothes will last and you won't have to spend as much time shopping. Then take a part of your savings and use it to help someone in your community who can't afford a home, car, credit cards, or clothes.

4. *Conserve your time.* Many years ago I met a busy executive who said his staff could keep him in meetings twenty-seven hours every day. When would he have any time to spend with his family? I asked him. He replied that he scheduled time to be with his family. You need to schedule your freedom or you will never have it. Limit your commitments. Frequently say, "No." View free time as valuable time. None of us are so valuable that we cannot take time off. Imagine if you had suddenly died. Are you so irreplaceable that you can't even take time off for dying?

ADDITIONAL QUOTES ON CONSERVATION ∞

Time is the coin of your life. It is the only coin you have, and only you can determine how it will be spent. Be careful lest you let other people spend it for you.

—CARL SANDBURG

_____

_____

_____

_____

_____

Beware of little expenses. A small leak will sink a great ship ... ere you consult your fancy, consult your purse.

—BEN FRANKLIN

_____

_____

_____

_____

_____

Half our life is spent trying to find something to do with the time we have rushed through life trying to save.

—WILL ROGERS

_____

_____

_____

_____

_____

We must use time creatively, and forever realize that the time is always ripe to do right.

—NELSON MANDELA

_____

_____

_____

_____

_____

THE SIXTH VIRTUE
Industry

"Lose no time," Franklin said. "Be always employed in something useful." Franklin retired from the printing business at forty-two, and for the next four years devoted himself to scientific research. Later he served America as a diplomat in England and France. He was continually involved in community service, developing a public library, fire department, police department, mail service, and hospital. Franklin developed the stove that bears his name and is still being manufactured today. He was offered a monopoly patent on the stove, but refused it and instead published a pamphlet describing how any blacksmith could produce it. Franklin donated his energy, ideas, and inventions to the American public.

By example, Franklin encouraged us to start working as soon as possible and to find work that will give us a feeling of accomplishment. Having satisfaction in our work is an inner attitude. It doesn't really matter what type of work we do or how much we accomplish. Instead, if we believe that what we are doing has a purpose, we will more likely maintain a positive attitude towards it—and ourselves. Then our achievements can have no limits.

Also, realize that the goal of Industry is to be productive. Once a women said to me, "What do smokestacks have to do with families?" I think she missed the point of this particular virtue and applied it to only nuts and bolts business applications. Actually it can also relate to being productive spiritually and at work, school, or in our homes. Industry might refer to improving a relationship. It might refer to contributing to a social cause. Without this virtue, many individuals may feel lost and disenfranchised. This is especially true in our inner cities where there is high unemployment. Young men and women need self-esteem based on real work.

There are so many things that need to be discovered and improved. The day is short, there is much work to be done, and often we don't have the motivation to get going. During the early 1900s, the director of the United States Patent Office approached President McKinley and suggested that the patent office be closed: "We have the telegraph, steamship, and railroad. After all, what more could possibly be invented?"

The world is sown with good; but unless I turn my glad thoughts into practical living and till my own field, I cannot reap a kernel of the good.

—HELEN KELLER

We often have good intentions and good thoughts toward other people. But, what good are words without action? Don't tell me how much you love me; show me! And you needn't make any flamboyant gestures. Ordinary actions can often have the greatest impact on others. For example, look how much happiness you can give a person by simply smiling "Hello."

A man who does not leave his hut will bring nothing in.

—WEST AFRICAN PROVERB

———————————

It is so easy to stay where you are. Home is so comfortable and familiar. But are you content or have you just settled for your present situation? If you do not go out, how will you improve? If you do not try something new, how will you advance yourself? If a salesman expects to make a sale, he needs to keep knocking on doors. So don't just sit still. Hustle. This proverb applies if your hut is in the rain forests of Brazil or on the top floor of Trump Tower in Manhattan.

Diligence is the Mother of Good Luck.

—BEN FRANKLIN

———————

Diligence means planning, long hours, and hard work. But there is also good luck, which often flavors the diligent because their work habits position them for a higher percentage of wins and successes. While they might appear to be making a gamble in business, their knowledge and experience have really made it a sure thing. With much thought and hard work, even what seems impossible becomes possible.

Our greatest weariness comes from work not done.

—ERIC HOFFER

A preoccupation with what needs to be done can overwhelm our thoughts, and we may blow an assignment or task completely out of proportion until it is actually worked on. Consider how much more relaxed you are after initiating and completing the work.

WHAT TO DO ❧

1. *When you start your day, ask yourself, "What good can I do today?"* Ben Franklin started each day early in the morning. Usually he was up by 5 A.M. He spent the early morning washing, meditating, and then resolving in his mind what he would do that day. This was a critical time because it set the tone and direction for the rest of his day. He would ask himself each morning: What Good shall I do this day? In the evening, just prior to going to sleep, he would ask the question: What Good have I done today? How would you answer these questions? These questions will give you an ideal to work towards and a satisfaction in accomplishment.

My question is what kind of alarm clock did Franklin use? Most of us are using clocks with snooze alarms. Some of these snooze alarms never seem to wake us up.

2. *We all need some encouragement and direction to maintain good work habits.* One of the worst problems that occurs with any business is wasting time. Talking on the phone, visiting with friends, long breaks, and basically not maintaining an interest at the workplace are all poor work habits. Good habits begin at home.

My children are glued to the couch when it comes to doing chores like washing dishes, doing yard work, and keeping their rooms clean. I am not doing them any good when I don't tell them how I expect things to be in our home.

3. *Once a week, turn off the television, if only for a few hours.* Watching television is a major cause of lost productivity. It is an addictive habit to come home and plop down in front of the TV set. Instead, use that time to read, go for a walk, visit a park with your child, visit a library or museum. or have a dinner with family and friends.

4. *You must act if you hope to accomplish anything.* You can only think so much. So how do you start? The simple work of greeting a person might start with the idea of wanting to be friends. Until you actually open your mouth, say hello, and put a sincere smile on your face, though, you have not accomplished anything.

5. *Examine your work habits daily.* Can things be improved? Often we get caught in repetitive ways of doing our work and come to believe there is no room for improvement. View change as a healthy way to make yourself more successful.

Seek out other people's viewpoints and advice, if necessary. In my small office I will encourage workers to help me in solving problems, and I continually try to improve the way we do things. Frustrating problems and difficult people can be viewed as an opportunity for improvement.

ADDITIONAL QUOTES ON INDUSTRY ∞

It's not enough to be busy ... the question is: what are we busy about?

—HENRY DAVID THOREAU

_____

_____

_____

_____

_____

Work spares us from three great evils: boredom, vice, and need.

—VOLTAIRE

_____

_____

_____

When you cease to make a contribution, you begin to die.

—ELEANOR ROOSEVELT

_____

_____

_____

Never let work drive you, master it and keep in complete control.

—BOOKER T. WASHINGTON

_____

_____

_____

Pride and laziness are the keys to poverty.

—HISPANIC PROVERB

_____

_____

_____

Sincerity

Franklin served as a diplomat in France from 1776 to 1785, during the years of the United States' infancy; and his success was not based on a contrived appearance or well-spun beliefs. He dressed casually and modestly. He was internationally known as a scientist and humorist, his humor serving to open doors and develop friendships with influential people. Franklin's wisdom, tact, and honesty were critical in developing relationships with European nations. He maintained his intellectual honesty and confidence in his own ability and mission. And Franklin wrote about the need—one still important today—for young people of honesty and integrity to help serve their country. In these ways, he practiced his belief that one should, "Think innocently and justly; and if you speak, speak accordingly." For how you speak reflects who you are.

Sincerity combines truthfulness with a concern for another person. So be direct, kind, and tactful when speaking, not misleading; and recognize how your words will affect those you are addressing. Then people will trust and confide in you. Also, act with sincerity. If I promise something to my children but don't deliver, I am teaching them it is okay to break promises and disappoint others. Finally, don't let other people's words convince you they are sincere, but depend on their good actions to show you how sincere and well-intentioned they are.

A little sincerity is a dangerous thing, and a great deal of it is absolutely fatal.

—OSCAR WILDE

———————————

Sincerity requires tact. Sometimes telling the truth can be brutal, so you should mix kindness with the truth when you tell it, otherwise your sincerity will be downright nasty. Once I heard a tale of a man who would only tell the truth. He attended the wedding of an extremely plain-looking bride. Many of the guests came up to her and congratulated her and wished her much happiness. He did so too, but he also told her, as truthfully as he could, how unattractive she looked on her wedding day. You can imagine how quickly he had to run in order to save his life. Although in his mind he was telling the truth, one might argue that he was giving an opinion. It is important that you don't confuse the two. You can avoid many conflicts by keeping unsolicited opinions to yourself.

Truth is mighty and will prevail. There is nothing the matter with this, except that it ain't so.

—MARK TWAIN

———————

In the long run—we like to believe—truth will rise up and prevail over falsehoods. Unfortunately this often takes time and patience, while falsehoods have a tendency to dominate and are often hard to eradicate. These falsehoods may also disguise themselves as truths. History books throughout the world are full of many revised accounts of what "really happened." And many of today's truths may be easily revised tomorrow. Racism, sexism, and anti-Semitism have been maintained for generations, and they still exist today despite countless seminars and voices speaking up against these hateful beliefs. The truth is often presented, but some people just aren't interested in listening.

I have tried to be honest. To be honest is to confront the truth. However unpleasant and inconvenient the truth may be, I believe we must expose and face it if we are to achieve a better quality of American life.

—MARTIN LUTHER KING, JR.

I need to take more responsibility for what I do. It is common for me to take the easy way out and pretend that I am doing the right thing. Often I will find myself rationalizing or making up excuses for my mistakes. I will cover up what I did. I will blame others for my errors. Confronting the truth requires honesty and action, as unpleasant as that may be.

You must speak straight so that your words may go like sunlight to our hearts.

—COCHISE OF THE APACHES

In difficult situations, I appreciate when I am told exactly where I stand. At times I may not be interested in hearing the truth; however, I would much prefer knowing the truth than being fed falsehoods. I find that the truth gives me a sense of calm. Now at least I can have more resolve to deal with problems and prepare for the future. Frequently patients may have a serious medical problem. I find the best policy is to speak straight to their hearts. At times a situation may appear bleak, but physicians cannot accurately predict the future, and it is not our job to remove any sense of hope.

WHAT TO DO ∞

1. *Monitor what you say and choose the right time to say it.* With your words you can ruin a friendship or create one. If you think that your words may hurt another person, make sure that what you have to say is not for personal gain and can be used constructively by the other person.

2. *When dealing with an explosive situation, ask yourself, "How would I like someone to speak to me about this?"* Even when you think you are saying something innocent, it may still blow up in your face. Sometimes I get a second opinion by consulting my wife on how to word things. There have been many times when I wrote down what I wanted to say, to make sure that I didn't say something I would regret. For example, I may jot down a few phrases on a note card and review it before I have an important meeting. Then, if I am anxious, reading the note will reassure me and calm me down.

3. *Don't be afraid of correcting yourself.* How do we know that we are really speaking the truth? Frequently we can be misled by our egos and think that we are in the right when we are definitely mistaken. In these situations, we have a responsibility to modify our position later, even if we feel ashamed. We will always make errors.

4. *Correct misunderstandings.* Despite our best intentions we may say insensitive things that cause another a great deal of pain. I think we have an obligation, after the smoke clears, to make an effort to bring peace back. A direct, in-person apology is more effective than a phone call that may be easily forgotten. In addition, writing a letter of apology solidifies what we sincerely mean. The letter gives us the opportunity to be careful in choosing our words and is something the reader can review.

ADDITIONAL QUOTES ON SINCERITY ∽

The truth is rarely pure and never simple.

—OSCAR WILDE

_____

_____

_____

_____

_____

To be persuasive, we must be believable. To be believable, we must be credible. To be credible, we must be truthful.

—EDWARD R. MURROW

_____

_____

_____

_____

_____

You can fool too many of the people too much of the time.

—JAMES THURBER

_____

_____

_____

One who digs a hole for another may fall in himself.

—RUSSIAN PROVERB

_____

_____

_____

Every truth has two sides. It is well to look at both, before we commit ourselves to either side.

—AESOP

_____

_____

_____

_____

_____

Justice

"Wrong none, by doing injuries or omitting the benefits that are your duty," Franklin wrote about being just. It was a virtue he grew to know well as a patriot and as a father. Franklin became a revolutionary in response to England's terrible treatment of the American colonies. He was enraged by England's arrogance and put his life on the line to make America free. To his regret and embarrassment, his son, William, sided with England. "Nothing," Franklin said, "has ever hurt me so much and affected me with such keen sensations, as to find myself deserted in my old age by my only son; and not only deserted, but to find him taking up arms against me, in a cause wherein my good fame, my fortune, and life were all at stake." Yet Franklin showed conciliation to his son by adding, "I ought not to blame you for differing in Sentiment with me in Public Affairs. We are Men, all subject to Errors."

Justice is a harsh term. It means one must determine a correct, unwavering path. In reality, you often judge others based on misinformation. So when dealing with friends, family, and business associates it is best to resist judging them. Give them the benefit of the doubt.

If you witness an injustice, try to understand more about it. Study it. Gather as much data as you can. Sense the "evil" that may be occurring. Be sensitive to the hurt, but do not react rashly or foolishly. Act within the law. If you don't act, in some way, however, then you are only adding to the injustice.

Every man must decide whether he will walk in the light of creative altruism or the darkness of destructive selfishness. This is the judgment. Life's most persistent and urgent question is, What are you doing for others.

—MARTIN LUTHER KING, JR.

———————

I am free to choose how I will act. Will I act justly? Will I choose to extend myself and reach out to another person and be a friend? Will I choose to ignore those around me and instead focus on my own inadequacy or selfish wants? There is so much that needs to be done. Just action is needed, not simply good intentions.

For example, after signing the Declaration of Independence, Franklin became increasingly disturbed about the continuation of slavery in America. Unlike so many who with their silence let slavery thrive, Franklin later served as president of the Pennsylvania Society for Promoting the Abolition of Slavery. And in the last months of his life, Franklin's final act was to petition Congress against slavery and the slave trade.

The possibility that we may fail in the struggle ought not to deter us from the support of a cause we believe to be just.

—ABRAHAM LINCOLN

————————————

There are always losers and winners in any fight. Unfortunately, you can't win all the time even though your odds of winning may look great; and if the odds of winning are against you, you may be reluctant to fight at all. So it takes commitment to back something in which you believe.

The highest result of education is tolerance.

—HELEN KELLER

A goal for each of us should be learning not just facts and figures but also how to work with other people. Ask yourself: Am I patient? Am I dogmatic? Can I maintain an open mind and listen to opinions with which I may disagree? Am I so convinced that I am right that I may be blinded to the correct path? Am I willing to learn from others? Do I leap to conclusions about other people's actions or ideas? Ask yourself: Am I treated poorly in return? You can't expect fair treatment unless you also treat others fairly.

How wonderful it is that nobody need wait a single moment before starting to improve the world.

—ANNE FRANK

———————————

I recall a story about a group of families who were crossing a bridge. Suddenly the bridge collapsed, and they all fell into the cold waters below. A farmer happened to be nearby, and he jumped in the water to rescue the people. With so many people screaming, it was unlikely he would be able to rescue them all. Nonetheless he dragged out one person at a time. Another person happened by and only watched. He told the farmer, "Why bother? You can't hope to save all of them." The farmer replied sharply, "Each person is valuable. I may not be able to save them all. But even one person is worth it. So don't waste my time talking. Help out now!"

There are times when even justice brings harm with it.

—SOPHOCLES

———————————

Justice often appears to be inflexible and insensitive. And there are times when it may cause more harm than good. For example, when we discipline a child, it takes a great deal of sensitivity as parents to do so such that the child learns and benefits from the experience. There is a fine line that we walk. If I am too harsh and inflexible, it may discourage the child. If I am acting too wishy-washy, as though the misdeed doesn't matter, the child may become more undisciplined. However, even when I believe I have thought things out in as fair a way as possible, it is not uncommon for me to later regret the way I handled the situation. With a sincere apology, my children usually rebound quickly from my harsh Justice.

WHAT TO DO ∞

1. *You have a responsibility to right any wrongs you may have done to another.* Swallow your pride, admit your mistakes, apologize, and reimburse others for any injury or damages that you may have caused them. Frequently I may get inappropriately upset over a small problem at home or work and become angry. I try to make a point to apologize to my wife, child, or coworker and try to make right any misunderstanding. A letter of retraction and apology is an excellent action. Contributing time to a community service program or giving money to a charity may also be a way to make amends.

2. *When you see an injustice occurring, get involved.* Simply writing a letter to a congressman or a newspaper may be an effective first step. You can protest or collect money for a charity or donate your time. We all have an obligation to help in some way to strengthen our community. Each situation you choose to be involved with, though, needs to be examined carefully to make sure you are not being pulled into the wrong camp. Read about the situation and discuss it as much as possible before you commit yourself.

3. *We need to develop closeness and trust with our local law enforcement officers to preserve our right to life, liberty, and the pursuit of happiness in our communities.* Most of them care deeply about fairness and want to maintain safe, decent neighborhoods. We can help them by alerting them to criminal activity, from drug dealing to domestic abuse.

4. *Practice focusing on your own slips and de-emphasize the actions of others.* Sometimes we can be pretty critical of other people. I try to give people the benefit of any doubts and to look at a person and his actions in a favorable light, but this takes a lot of practice. Some people are very obnoxious, and it can be hard at times to show sympathy for them. Fair treatment of others requires having more tolerance for their errors and mistakes. Franklin talked about keeping your eyes wide open when selecting a spouse, but maintaining a sleepy eye when you are married. He meant that a relationship needs to have quite a bit of flexibility and tolerance for it to maintain peace and success. Harsh judgments and an attitude of "You should have done . . ." will lead to failure.

5. *A strong fist does not equal justice.* We all need to remember this every day, and encourage our children to do so also. As adults we need to restrain ourselves from hitting young children. Firm scolding, silent stares, and time-out are examples of how we can discipline children without having to harm them. In addition, when children use hitting as a rationale for settling disputes, they need to be told in a kind yet firm way to keep their hands to themselves. They shouldn't be allowed to believe that the violence in movies and television is normal.

By fifteen years of age, the average child has witnessed thousands of murders and countless acts of violence and rape on television. We need to oppose media violence through education, organizations, and legislation, and set limits on what children watch at home and at the movies.

6. *Make our schools and neighborhoods safe areas again.* Guns and weapons are an increasing problem in our schools and cities. Playground fights that used to end in bloody noses now end with a gunshot and are often fatal. We need to aggressively oppose these problems.

ADDITIONAL QUOTES ON JUSTICE ∽

When you are right you cannot be too radical, when you are wrong you cannot be too conservative.

—MARTIN LUTHER KING, JR.

_____

_____

_____

_____

_____

Where, after all, do universal human rights begin? In small places, close to home—so close and so small that they cannot be seen on any map of the world. Yet they are the world of the individual person, the neighborhood he lives in, the school or college he attends, the factory, farm or office where he works. Such are the places where every man, woman and child seeks equal justice, equal opportunity, equal dignity without discrimination. Unless these rights have meaning there, they have little meaning anywhere.

—ELEANOR ROOSEVELT

Recompense injury with justice, and recompense kindness with kindness.

—CONFUCIUS

_____

_____

_____

A wrong done to one man is a wrong done to all men.

—FREDERICK DOUGLASS

_____

_____

_____

No act of kindness, no matter how small, is ever wasted.

—AESOP

_____

_____

_____

_____

_____

Moderation

Franklin once told a parable about a man who did not share a garden tool with his brothers, earning him a great deal of resentment and hard feelings. One brother, however, did not show any obvious resentment and later demonstrated his generous side to his stingy brother by loaning him an important tool. Similarly, as a politician and diplomat, Franklin frequently ran across nasty, self-serving individuals with whom he still had to negotiate and maintain civil relations. From these experiences, Franklin learned to "avoid extremes . . . and resenting injuries."

All the virtues listed by Franklin should be done with moderation. Any virtue in extreme can cause problems. A person who is too industrious at their occupation may neglect their family and friends. If I am too sensitive, I may get upset over minor disagreements, and if I am not sensitive enough, I may be oblivious to serious difficulties. Balance is a critical component to successfully develop character.

It is interesting that Franklin did not choose patience as one of his virtues.

I think he was anxious to see immediate improvement in the way he was. I tend to be impatient and easily get frustrated waiting for a garden to grow and give its fruits. It is often easy for me to tell someone to be patient, but it is another thing for me to sit and wait. I've found that I can relieve my impatience by starting a new project. Perhaps Franklin, who had no shortage of projects, felt the same way.

Keep your eyes on the stars and your feet on the ground.

—THEODORE ROOSEVELT

Dream for the future. By reaching for the stars, it is less likely you will be standing in mud. Look ahead and make goals for yourself, then strive, sweat, and sacrifice to accomplish them. Act with caution, though, and balance your dreams with common sense. Recognize what you must give up to achieve them, and consider if the dreams are worth it.

There is a folktale about a cobbler who dreamed that under a certain bridge in a certain town was a box with a treasure of gold. The dream would haunt him each night, and finally after many sleepless nights, he took off on a journey to this far off town. When he reached the spot, he noticed there was a guard watching the bridge. Many hours passed, and finally the cobbler could not stand it and began to dig for his treasure. The guard approached him and interrogated him. When the guard heard the story of treasure, he began to laugh and said, "You foolish man. I had the same dream of gold in a box, buried near a hearth in a cobbler's home in a far off town. If we all pursued our dreams, the world would be full of disappointed men." When the cobbler heard this story, he rushed home to find a box of gold buried near his hearth.

Patience and diligence, like faith, remove mountains.

—WILLIAM PENN

Patience and diligence require a lot of inner strength. Often, serious problems cannot be solved overnight. It may take you months and even years to find a solution, but great obstacles can be overcome with hard work. The Wright Brothers worked for years before finally flying, and did so during a time when few people could even conceive of airplanes. Who would have imagined then that men would someday also walk on the moon?

Slow and steady wins the race.

—AESOP

———————

Consistency and caution can be major keys to success. The person who lives according to his means and gradually saves money each month will in the end be doing very well financially. Stories about quickly made fortunes and high-risk investments that pay off big may make the papers frequently, but the investor who is systematic, circumspect, and smart is more likely to create a fortune, although it may take many years. It is amazing how much we can accomplish or learn if we devote only a few minutes each day to a task or to study.

Through anger, the truth looks simple.

—JANE McCABE

———————

When I am angry my thoughts may not be clear and I may distort what is happening. I have a tendency to reduce things to simple terms. But the truth is rarely black and white; more likely it has shades of gray. Often I will get into a disagreement with my children and misunderstand what they want (they have a tendency to be demanding at times). However, as a parent I may need to make a quick decision that is not very popular and only excerbates the problem. Fortunately a few days later, after I've given matters some additional thought, I may come up with a compromise that proves to be a winner. A common problem is picking a time to send my children to bed. Because my children are different ages, one time may not be appropriate for the other. Thus, I'm very familiar with the expression, "Not fair!" Even I get confused over this. Some nights I have to be the dictator and declare, "Enough! Turn off the TV now. It is time to stop the noise. Read and get ready for bed." I am always reworking this one, and I hope one day to get it solved.

WHAT TO DO ∞

1. *Put happiness in perspective.* There are many wonderful things in the world for us to enjoy. For balance, though, we need to remember that we won't have all the time in the world to enjoy them. There was once a sage who carried a piece of paper in one pocket on which was written, "All in the world was made for my use." In his other pocket was a note that said, "I am only food for the worms."

2. *We should not bear grudges against others.* Small problems can become overblown, pride too easily can get in the way of good relations, and arrogance can unbalance relationships. Often, at home labor may not seem evenly divided, and this can serve as a point of contention. We need to beware of the attitude, "This is for me to do and that is for you to do." This attitude can too easily deteriorate into "What have you done for me?" I often remind myself, "What can I do for my wife to make her happy?" This may involve cleaning dishes, yard work, child care, car pooling, or caring for elderly parents. This attitude is a tasty medicine that prevents struggles and grudges.

3. *Begin saving in your youth, and save a few dollars each day.* With the magic of compound interest and the help of time, the savings will gradually grow into a sizable fortune. Many people do not realize that small amounts of savings consistently invested over time will result in sizable returns. Also spend some time learning about investing.

4. *Make a vice into a virtue.* Anger and pride are vices that can be virtues when used in moderation. Being angry when an injustice occurs will help motivate you to make changes and correct the injustice. And pride reminds you that you can—and should—feel good about yourself when you succeed. But left unchecked, these vices can be devastating and ruin your reputation and relationships. Having a hair-trigger personality that explodes with minor problems only causes hurt feelings and may lead to potentially violent situations. And too much pride may lead you to act unwisely and unjustly.

5. *If you are angry, walk away.* Don't use stinging words or sarcasm that will hurt the person who upsets you. Definitely don't use your fists. Instead, go to another room or out for a walk. Return in fifteen or thirty minutes, or when you feel calmer and can discuss the problem in a more rational way. It is amazing how a few minutes will put things in perspective.

ADDITIONAL QUOTES ON MODERATION ∾

If you desire many things, many things will seem but a few.

—BEN FRANKLIN

_____

_____

_____

_____

_____

All music jars when the soul's out of tune.

—CERVANTES

_____

_____

_____

_____

_____

Heat not a furnace for your foe so hot
That it do singe yourself.

—SHAKESPEARE

_____

_____

_____

_____

_____

The archer that shoots over, misses as much as he that falls short.

—MONTAIGNE

_____

_____

_____

_____

_____

Health

"Tolerate no uncleanness in body, cloths, or habitation," Franklin said. Franklin frequently wrote about and practiced eating and exercising in moderation to maintain his good health. For most of his life, he was generally free of illness. In his later years he did suffer from gout, a metabolic disorder, and kidney stones, illnesses that severely restricted his activities and often left him bedridden; but despite the severe, chronic pain, he maintained a cheerful disposition. I have met many patients who have also maintained positive and often humorous attitudes despite severe disabilities. Their positive attitudes seem to lessen the pain and impact of the illness. This is a major challenge that most of us will have to face. Fortunately there are many friends and professionals who can assist us. We often need to be reminded that we are not alone.

Health may also relate to self-improvement. None of us are perfect. All of us have traits and bad habits that can be worked on and improved. Franklin frequently wrote about the image of a garden with plants and weeds that need some cultivation. Just as we set aside time to brush our teeth, we can also set aside time to reexamine ourselves and make ourselves better individuals. A good time to cultivate a garden in your children is when they are very young. This may prevent the garden from being overgrown with weeds as they become older.

We often overlook our good health until we get sick. So we should do what we can now to prevent illness, including eating in moderation and exercising on a regular basis. Consider the extreme cost of health care. By acting preventively, we will also contribute to our own future financial security. And habits like smoking, drinking, and using drugs are hard to break. It is much easier not to start. "Just say no" seems a superficial solution, however. Usually stress, unhappiness, social pressure, and lack of opportunities serve as the source for addictive habits. It often takes a great deal of courage not to start bad habits, but it is even more difficult dealing with the sources.

A man's habit clings and he will wear tomorrow what today he wears.

—EDNA ST. VINCENT MILLAY

Our day is comprised of routines, and it is hard to break from these and follow new paths. Thus, if you pick up habits, it is better to pick up good ones. A regime of daily walking or reading will give you much enjoyment. Smoking, however, will quietly destroy your life. I was taught that when giving charity, it is better to give small amounts each week rather than giving only a large amount once or twice a year. The habit of doing it regularly makes it a part of your nature.

Health is not a condition of matter, but of Mind.

—MARY BAKER EDDY

So much of your health depends on your attitude and spirit. If you are filled with grim thoughts, you may not value your life and may as well be near death. With discouraging thoughts, you can turn a temporary situation over time into permanent depression. I have seen many patients with poor attitudes crippled by their diseases that offer no opportunity for improvement. I have also seen patients with horrible problems maintain a positive attitude. They say to me, "I know a lot of people that are worse off than me," or, "It could have been a lot worse than it was." These people inevitably have a better chance for recovery.

The first wealth is health.

—RALPH WALDO EMERSON

For the most part, children and young adults tend to take their good health for granted, but I know many elderly patients who would trade all their wealth to shed themselves of their chronic illnesses. They spent most of their lives sedentary and overweight, and now they have severe arthritis of the hips and ankles and are in constant pain with restricted movements. Possibly if they had exercised moderately and maintained a more ideal body weight, they would have had fewer problems. Now they have trouble walking up steps. Getting dressed and getting out of bed are often painful chores. Simple preventative measures such as eating in moderation, exercising regularly, maintaining a good humor, getting enough sleep, and scheduling free time can insure your first wealth.

A good garden may have some weeds.

—THOMAS FULLER, M.D.

I often look at myself in a positive light and overlook my defects. My personality traits are sometimes weak and need improvement. I become angry at the wrong time. I am not appreciative of what people have done for me. Just like a garden has some weeds, we all have weaknesses that need rooting out.

No gains without pains.

—BEN FRANKLIN

Imagine the frustrations you might feel if you are trying to lose weight and everyone else in your home is eating ice cream and cake. It is not easy following a regular program of improvement, especially alone. For us to make any change requires some support from friends and family members. We need to continually remember that we do not have to be traveling alone. There are close people who can assist us and make a painful change more tolerable.

The expression "No pain, no gain" is often applied to sports. If I want to get better at playing basketball, I am going to have to practice. The mastery of piano takes many years. If I want to make myself a better person, it will take time and work. It doesn't happen overnight, however, I can begin today.

WHAT TO DO ∽

1. *Eat in moderation and focus on a vegetarian-based, high-carbohydrate, low-fat diet.* Make regular aerobic exercise a priority. Walk twenty to thirty minutes four times per week. Other good aerobic activities include bicycle riding, jogging, and swimming. Get at least six to nine hours of sleep each night.

2. *Practice waking up each morning and saying, "What a great day it is and what a great person I am."* Maintaining good health also entails having a positive attitude and a good feeling for oneself. How is this done? Say to yourself, "I have many things to be grateful for." Repeat this statement each day; it may soon set the tone for your days, your weeks, and your years.

3. *Visit a hospital or nursing home.* Many of us have a tendency to forget that we have strong hands and stable feet, strong eyes and keen hearing, and countless other physical abilities that make our life a pleasure. This exercise will let you appreciate your good fortune—and give you the opportunity to share it with others who have to suffer without it.

4. *In a sexual relationship, be responsible or be sorry.* Today, sexual permissiveness is irresponsible behavior. HIV infection is a world-wide epidemic, and there is no way for us to tell by looking at someone if they are HIV positive. We often get complacent and don't realize that any new sexual encounter could be a time bomb. Maintaining a monogamous relationship or abstinence are the only sure guarantees you will avoid HIV infection.

5. *To begin making changes, begin today.* As a physician I have seen many patients with poor eating and exercise habits. They all admit that it is good to eat properly and to exercise regularly. After discussing the benefits of making a change and having a discussion on how to start, the majority leave the office with good intentions but never change their habits. To make any change, no matter how small, is a difficult task which requires a major commitment by the patient. Many of us fall into the habit of saying, "Not today, but I will have time tomorrow." But perhaps you will never have time tomorrow.

6. *Keep a clear head.* Smoking, alcohol, and illegal drugs are things that you can choose to use or not use. If you want to maintain a healthy body and a clear mind, however, these drugs need to be used sparingly or not at all. Smoking is clearly an addiction with many serious long-term adverse health effects. Alcohol, used frequently and excessively, can result in serious medical and social problems. Illegal psychoactive drugs can have subtle and major addictive tendencies and with frequent use can have multiple, irreversible toxic effects. Often, use of these substances is started only because of social pressure, fueled by the need to belong and not to be different. These foolish actions detract from your health and your success.

ADDITIONAL QUOTES ON HEALTH ∞

Health and appetite impart the sweetness to sugar, bread and meat.

—RALPH WALDO EMERSON

_____

_____

_____

_____

_____

There is only one corner of the universe you can be certain of improving, and that's your own self.

—ALDOUS HUXLEY

_____

_____

_____

_____

_____

There is a limit to the best of health: disease is always a near neighbor.

—AESCHYLUS

_____

_____

_____

If a child comes to school hungry, the best school in the world won't help.

—ARTHUR ASHE

_____

_____

_____

Think excitement, talk excitement, act excitement, and you are bound to be an excited person.

—NORMAN VINCENT PEALE

_____

_____

_____

_____

_____

THE ELEVENTH VIRTUE
Calmness

"Don't be disturbed by trifles or at unavoidable or common accidents," wrote Franklin, who was noted for his calmness. He was the oldest delegate to the Constitutional Convention, which met in 1787 to plan a government for the United States. Each of the states had special interests that created major disagreements between them. Franklin's presence, humor, and tact served to soothe many of the tempers, so the members could stay on track. Fulfilling his dream of a unified country required a cool head.

Maintaining calmness at home and work is a good goal. In a calm atmosphere we will usually feel relaxed, and this will help us improve our ability to function. We can show kindness more easily. We may also be more thoughtful and creative. The greatest threat to calmness may be a busy schedule; a shortage of time may make us short in our temper, so all our schedules should include some free time and moments for reflection.

Anger is a natural emotion that can have a variety of textures. Anger should be responsibly expressed without insulting the other person. It can also be helpful in motivating us to correct an injustice. Ideally anger should be demonstrated only over important matters that can motivate others to act in a proper way. If I act on my anger immediately, often I end up regretting the way I acted. It is best to swallow my anger at a particular moment and let it pass. Over time, either in minutes or days, a situation can be examined more calmly and a peaceful solution arrived at. Usually it is helpful to have a disagreement privately. This is especially useful when disciplining a child.

He is poor who does not feel content.

—JAPANESE PROVERB

———————————

We often do not appreciate what we have. We may not be able to see it all, or we may want more. Frequently we think that money or possessions will give us satisfaction and happiness. There is an old question: Who is rich? Usually we will answer, a man with lots of money or possessions. Instead consider this answer: A man who is happy with what he has. Part of contentment is appreciating what is occurring. When the rain falls, we may view it as an inconvenience. However, the rain nourishes the fields, the grass grows, the cow feeds on the grass, and milk is made. So, actually milk is rain. I love it when it rains.

When a man angers you, he conquers you.

—TONI MORRISON

_____

When I happen to run into a demanding, angry person, I am calmed by a story about a boy who kicked his dog. One day a manager was pressured by his boss to produce. The manager yelled at his secretary, and the secretary was short with the receptionist. The receptionist came home that evening and told her son sharply to stop being so lazy. The boy then kicked the dog. Actually, a lot of bad energy could have been saved if the boss had walked into that home and kicked the dog himself.

Discontent is the first step in the progress of a man or a nation.

—OSCAR WILDE

———————————

Frustrations, bad luck, or tough situations can often be turned into opportunities for learning or success. I have met many people that have been fired from their jobs and have become extremely depressed. As it turns out, many of them use these opportunities to change careers or directions, and they often find better positions. Like many of us, Ben Franklin had trouble with his vision in his middle years. He was frustrated fumbling around with two sets of glasses when reading. This motivated him to invent the bifocal glasses that we still are using today.

It is easy to fly into a passion—anybody can do that—but to be angry with the right person to the right extent and at the right time and with the right object and in the right way—that is not easy, and it is not everyone who can do it.

—ARISTOTLE

We often get angry over minor things. Trivial disagreements are often forgotten quickly, but they result in quick words of hate and pain that may stay with us for years. If you become angry, use your anger in a thoughtful, controlled way and as a tool to achieve a goal. It takes wisdom and strength to express anger at the right time and in the right words, but it can be done with practice and patience. Recall how disappointed and angry Ben Franklin was when his son William opposed him during the Revolutionary War. Nevertheless, Franklin made clear his concerns in as kind a way as possible.

WHAT TO DO ∞

1. *Be content with what you have.* This requires some imagination. Focus on what is valuable to you, such as free time, visiting with family and friends, or education. How many successful businessmen are lying in their deathbeds, wishing that they had spent more time making business deals and regret the time they spent with their children?

2. *Take charge of your anger.* Raging uncontrollably is unacceptable behavior. Express anger when talking to other people without insulting or attacking them. Avoid blaming, accusing and fault finding, and express anger responsibly and positively. Instead of saying, "You are lazy and no good," say, "I am angry with you because you didn't clean up your room when you said you would." Your anger may be justified, but that doesn't justify hurting someone in return.

3. *Look for a middle ground and try to compromise instead of expecting things to always go your way.* Avoid absolute demands and try not to be inflexible and controlling. Rarely are we able to get all that we want when resolving a dispute. There may have to be some give-and-take until an equitable agreement is reached. It sometimes takes a great deal of thought and strategy to reach a peaceful outcome.

4. *Don't force yourself to be calm all the time.* Chronically suppressed anger may lead to illness and depression. Healthy outlets for anger include physical exercise, gardening, wood chopping, taking a long walk, or playing music. Express your feelings and let your friends know what behavior caused you to get upset. Explain what they can do to correct their behavior in the future: "I am angry with you because . . . and I would like you to do . . ." Or "I sat for an hour waiting for you. You did not call me to warn me that you would be late. Next time call me as soon as you know you will be late."

5. *Expect the worst and it probably won't happen.* There are often events that we don't have much control over, such as a car that won't start, bad weather, a computer crash, a sudden illness, or a drive-by shooting. Often we can prepare ourselves for the worst with all sorts of backup insurance, but even the most prepared of us are sometimes surprised by bad circumstances. I try to view these frustrations as a challenge. How will I perform under such difficult times? Usually the apparent problem turns out not to be too damaging. I recall a patient who would frequently imagine that she would shortly be suffering from an intractable cancer. I think she believed that if she prepared herself now for this imaginary disaster, it would never occur, and if it did happen, she would face it calmly.

6. *Correct with kindness.* Frequently one of my own children does a selfish, thoughtless act, and I think they need some attitude adjustment. I will be careful and correct them in an angry tone, but I put off disciplining them until a later time so that I can cool down. I remind myself to 'stay calm— and fake the anger later. Then after I correct them I try to speak to them firmly and kindly so they realize that I have their best interests at heart.

ADDITIONAL QUOTES ON CALMNESS ∞

If you are bitter at heart, sugar in the mouth will not help you.

—YIDDISH PROVERB

_____

_____

_____

_____

_____

Keep cool: anger is not an argument.

—DANIEL WEBSTER

_____

_____

_____

Up jumps the hare when you least expect it.

—HISPANIC PROVERB

_____

_____

_____

I've dealt with many crises in my life, but few will ever happen.

—MARK TWAIN

_____

_____

_____

_____

_____

Friendship

Ben Franklin said, "Protect your and other persons peace and reputation." He was noted for his benevolent nature. He had many friends because he was such a good friend.

Toward the last years of his life, Franklin returned to Philadelphia from France to live with his daughter, Sally. She nursed and pampered him. Often he remained in bed because of his severe pain; however, he frequently received visitors with joy and good humor. He could have so easily remained isolated and self-pitying, but Franklin viewed friendship as critical to the environment of life.

The famous naval commander John Paul Jones confided to Franklin about being abandoned by his friends. Franklin wrote to him with kind advice: "On occasion give your officers and friends a little more praise than is their due. Criticizing and censuring almost everyone you have to do with, will diminish friends, increase enemies, and thereby hurt your affairs."

Do not manipulate others or use someone for selfish reasons. Many times people associate with others for the wrong reason. Look beyond the surface for good qualities in people. Are they easy to be with? Are they kind? Are they sincere? Are they slow to anger? Or are they lazy? Do they complain? Are they always cutting people down? Choose your friends based on good qualities. These friendships tend to last.

It does take some effort and planning to be a friend. Franklin told a story of a political opponent who had spoken against him. Franklin was determined to be his friend. With some clever planning, Franklin asked to borrow a book from him, quickly returned it within a week, and enclosed a note of profound thanks. Within a few weeks this person changed his opinion and greeted Franklin in a kind way, and soon after they began a life-long friendship. Later Franklin said that this was "Another instance of the truth of the maxim, 'He that has once done you a kindness will be more ready to do yet another than he whom you yourself have obliged.' "

Friendships can be built on a strong foundation by showing respect and kindness. I heard a story of two young girls who became close friends in a death camp. They shared a single bowl and always shared their daily soup equally. Despite such a grim time, this extraordinary friendship flourished. Possibly their friendship kept them alive more than the miserable soup.

Be slow in choosing a friend, slower in changing.

—BEN FRANKLIN

A friend is someone to confide in, someone who will help shoulder your most difficult problems. Look for a person who will have your best interests at heart and will act accordingly. Friendships usually do not occur overnight. Trust develops only over time, but it's time well spent. One good friend is precious. Put energy into maintaining the friendship, and don't give up on it easily.

Friendship with oneself is all important, because without it one cannot be friends with anyone else in the world.

—ELEANOR ROOSEVELT

Wake up each morning with a positive attitude and view yourself in a good way. Be grateful for all that you have. For if you can only focus on your bad qualities, how can you possibly recognize other people's good qualities? And how can they appreciate yours? Good qualities might include calmness, dependability, kindness, cheerfulness, charity, and helpfulness. These virtues make our personal interactions a pleasure.

A true friend is the most precious of all possessions and the one we take the least thought about acquiring.

—LA ROCHEFOUCAULD

During good times, we will often have many friends, but a true friend presents himself during difficult times. Often he might not have been thought of as a friend until later, when we appreciate how his actions have helped us. He is more valuable than all the "good guys" we know.

Do not use a hatchet to remove a fly from your friend's forehead.

—CHINESE PROVERB

Use tact when you speak to your friend. If he is in trouble, use caution in giving him advice and help. Sometimes our advice is not wanted, and it may cause more harm than good. We may try to understand and empathize with his pain, but often we will not feel it. A better strategy, then, is just to listen.

WHAT TO DO ∽

1. *Focus on helping friends rather than taking from them.* Sharing your time with other people is the best way to be friends. Invite them over for brunch over the weekend. Inquire about their interests and goals. What have they recently accomplished? What problems are they encountering? How can you help out? Recall the virtue Silence, and listen carefully. Treat them the way you would want to be treated.

2. *See people for their virtues.* There is a fable that says we were made with two eyes for a special reason. With our weaker, less critical eye we focus on our friends and see mainly their good qualities. With our stronger eye, we look inside ourselves and see our own weaknesses and try to improve them. Often I catch myself doing the opposite. It is easy to overlook my own deficiencies. Fortunately my wife, who is also my friend, points them out when I act too obnoxious.

3. *We need to honor each person we encounter.* This applies to relatives, in-laws, spouses, and children. Too often we show respect to complete strangers and ignore those closest to us. In essence, we need to view each person with a good eye.

Speaking positively with compliments and encouragement scores a lot of points compared to criticism and cut-downs. Mundane things at home, such as cleaning the dishes, taking out the garbage, yard work, laundry, and picking up in the bedroom, serve as opportunities to give positive feedback. Nobody likes doing these ordinary tasks without hearing encouraging words. Words of encouragement can inspire a person to exceed expectations. Winston Churchill did poorly in school, however, one teacher said he saw a lot of good potential. Winston never forgot those words.

4. *Friendship can be extended to children.* Today, children are also involved in busy schedules and are stressed-out. Often parents don't have much time to be with their children, and many families are single-parent families and need extra help and support. You can help by volunteering as a Big Brother/Sister or by being involved in scouts or coaching. Children need mentors to model themselves after—and they can teach adults many things in return. Also spend less time watching your child play sports. Schedule time at home just being with them. Play quiet board games, such as checkers, Monopoly, or Sorry. Read to your child each night.

ADDITIONAL QUOTES ON FRIENDSHIP ∽

You cannot shake hands with a clenched fist.

—INDIRA GANDHI

Your friend is the man who knows all about you and still wants to be your friend.

—ELBERT HUBBARD

_____

_____

_____

I have found the paradox that if I love until it hurts, then there is no hurt, but only more love.

—MOTHER TERESA

_____

_____

_____

The only justification for ever looking down on somebody is to pick them up.

—JESSE JACKSON

_____

_____

_____

Treat all people as if they were related to you.

—NAVAJO PROVERB

_____

_____

_____

Modesty

When Franklin first developed his list of virtues, he left out modesty. A friend pointed out to him that his speech was often argumentative and pompous. Franklin wrote, "I was not content with being right when discussing any point, but was overbearing and insolent." Franklin worked on this virtue by modifying the way he spoke. He focused on not contradicting others, respecting their opinions, and trying to be less forceful and abrasive when asserting his own opinions. He avoided dogmatic expressions. He often got his point across by asking questions.

Franklin was convinced that if a person had enough money to live in comfort, he should devote the rest of his resources for the good of the community. Franklin told a story of a friend who showed him through a magnificent home. Franklin would ask, "Why would you want this room so large?" His friend would reply, "Because I can afford it." Each room would be larger than the next, and each time the reply was, "Because I can afford it." Eventually Franklin sharply said, "Why are you wearing such a small hat, why not get one ten times the size of your head? You can afford that too."

Being modest does not refer to weakness and non-assertiveness. A modest person might let his actions speak rather than his words. Modesty needs to be balanced with a healthy sense of who we are, of knowing our strengths and weaknesses. If we feel comfortable with ourselves, we don't have to blow a big horn to get attention. A person with a modest mind-set does not need to wear fancy designer clothing or drive a status-symbol automobile. Franklin both spoke and dressed modesty, but he was fully aware of his accomplishments and achievements. I still am overwhelmed when I realize how much he did for the good of his community and country. As a scientist and inventor, he came up with a number of commercially profitable devices, but never made an effort to protect them, giving them away to the public instead. Franklin lived his daily motto: "What Good shall I do today." He devoted his life for doing good for his friends. His friends included his community and country.

If I am not for myself, who will be for me? And if I am only for myself, what am I?

—HILLEL

———————————

A person with poor self-esteem faces a major struggle in work and relationships with other people. If you put little value in yourself, others will not value you, nor will they want to be with you. For if you are self-centered and don't have any real concern for others, you will be of little value to your community. And if a person has positive feelings about himself, they need to be balanced by a concern for other people. So be modest, but in moderation.

We should take care not to make the intellect our god; it has of course powerful muscles, but no personality.

———————————

What are we doing with all our knowledge and technology? Where has it led us? Is this generation any more advanced and civilized than previous ones? Scientific advances can be impressive and overwhelming, and we can easily be enticed by their elegance and power, but they are not the end-all-be-all of civilization. Often we are falsely led to believe that with scientific advances we can end poverty and war. Science does not put us above human compassion. Technology cannot replace a warm embrace. Character development is just as great a place to put our research and development dollars.

Whenever Nature leaves a hole in a person's mind, she generally plasters it over with a thick coat of self-conceit.

—HENRY WADSWORTH LONGFELLOW

Frequently we may cover up our fears and weaknesses with airs of confidence. Actually when I encounter a person who is arrogant and demanding, I begin thinking about how this negative trait will impact on him and interfere with his success. There is an ancient question: Who is wise? Most of us would answer a wise person is someone who knows a lot of stuff and can teach others. However, consider this: A wise person is someone who can learn from anyone. He can learn from a great teacher and he can learn from a child. Arrogance interferes with our ability to communicate and learn from people. How often do we run across a person who seems to have all the answers? Recall how often they are wrong.

Everybody can be great. Because anybody can serve.

—MARTIN LUTHER KING, JR.

———————————

The essence of modesty is contributing to the community. All of us have the potential to be helpful, provided we leave our huts and reach out. I may serve someone a meager glass of water and although the water has a minimal value to me, the service may have a profound effect for another beyond what I might understand today. We do not have to have special skills or resources to contribute. We need only to make it a priority in our minds and then act by being involved. Even if we contribute only an hour a week, it can be helpful.

WHAT TO DO ∞

1. Be less argumentative in speech and less openly critical of other people's opinions. Let people say what they want to say without interrupting them, then disagree if you do. Avoid phrases such as "You are wrong" or "What an idiotic idea." Instead say, "I respect your opinion, however . . ." or "My opinion is . . ."

2. Recognize that our gifts of thinking and creating can leave us at any moment. When we are young we often feel so invincible, but human life is very fragile. How many individuals thought that they were on easy street with lots of money when a sudden reversal cast them into a life of poverty or severe illness? Daily reminders of our vulnerability can change an arrogant attitude. My youngest daughter, Rebecca, was having exceptional success in school, and I was sensing that she was developing some arrogance in the way she spoke to her older brother. I realized that arrogance is a major hurdle for some people to overcome. If left unchecked, it can destroy a person.

3. Give back to your community. Many successful people believe that the money and property they have are not theirs—but are for safekeeping, to be used prudently for the benefit of those less fortunate in the world. The need to give back something to society and a feeling of indebtedness to society are healthy attitudes to foster. Contributing time or money to charities, religious groups, and social organizations on a regular basis are a few ways you can give back to society.

4. *Be sensitive to the tone of your voice.* Speak softly and slowly. It is amazing how softly spoken words are often heard more clearly than harsh loud words. Even if you don't speak, your facial expressions will tip off what your internal feelings really are. Recently my daughter's feelings were hurt by a friend. "It wasn't what she said that hurt. It was the way she rolled her eyes."

ADDITIONAL QUOTES ON MODESTY ∽

The noisiest drum has nothing in it but air.

—ENGLISH PROVERB

_____

_____

_____

_____

_____

Pride is said to be the last vice the good man gets clear of.

—BEN FRANKLIN

_____

_____

_____

We are all worms, but I do believe that I am a glowworm.

—WINSTON CHURCHILL

_____

_____

_____

The hurricane does not uproot grasses, which are pliant and bow low before it on every side. It is only the lofty trees that it attacks.

—PANCHATANTRA

_____

_____

_____

_____

_____

The greatest deception men suffer is from their own opinions.

—LEONARDO DA VINCI

_____

_____

_____

_____

_____

Appendix
10 *Ways* *to* *Use* The Road *to* Virtue *in the* Classroom

1. Make up a bulletin board entitled "What Good Shall I Do Today?" Begin each morning with this question. Do we have a list of things to do? How can we prioritize our list? What good deeds did the students do yesterday? What are examples of problems that still need to be solved?

2. Pick a quotation from *The Road to Virtue* and place it on the blackboard each week. Discuss it with the class for a few minutes. Have the children discuss what they think it may mean. Have them define the words or terms used in the quotation.

3. Writing assignments in English classes can focus on a particular virtue. For example, children could write their own fables or poetry. History is replete with individuals that may illustrate particular virtues. Discuss famous Americans and men and women from other cultures, focusing not just on what they accomplished but on what kind of people they were.

4. Analyze characters in novels or stories in terms of virtues that they used. What virtues may have made them more successful?

5. Remind your students that you are also a student of the virtues, then illustrate a virtue by discussing a problem that you have dealt with. Examples might be problems with an investment, disagreement with a teenager or parent, a past problem in your own teenage years, a financial or emotional reversal, or a prolonged illness. Then elicit similar stories from your students. Just as you are a role model for them, they can also teach you.

6. Invite a parent to the classroom to discuss a virtue that they value. Invite a local politician, business person, or member of the clergy to the classroom and have the guest discuss Justice, Sincerity, Honesty, or Conservation. How do they manage a busy schedule? How do they find time for their families or personal interests? Do they have role models or mentors?

7. Read aloud to the children for a few minutes. Pick stories that have good lessons and relate to virtues. Then discuss the children's reactions.

8. Find simple examples and ways that a child can make connections with the virtues in their own life—at school and at home. Often, a child in the classroom will make suggestions to you. Virtues can be found and applied in all subject matter, including music, art, science, and physical education.

9. Virtues need to be exercised with balance. Give examples of people being excessively virtuous and how that caused serious problems.

10. In secondary schools, *The Road to Virtue* can supplement existing programs on health maintenance, conflict resolution, occupational training, counseling, substance abuse, teenage pregnancy, and leadership training. Analyze a community service, class, or fundraising project. Look at the good and bad points of the project. How were the virtues properly or improperly used to complete it?

For other learning materials and training for the classroom, contact:

Franklin Center for Character Development
17500 Medical Center Parkway, Suite 6
Independence, Missouri 64057
(800) 241-9770

How did you use *The Road to Virtue*? How did this book affect you? Are there any special quotations or ideas you would like to share with me? Please share your thoughts by writing to me at:

Michael L. Loren, M.D.
17500 Medical Center Parkway
Independence, Missouri 64057

or by E-mail:

Mloren@aol.com